How to Get a State Job

MICHELLE S. ALLEN

ISBN: 145285534X
ISBN-13: 9781452855349

About the author:

This book is designed to demystify the process of applying for civil service jobs in the State of California.

A graduate of California State University Sacramento, Michelle Allen started with The State Department of Education and finished her state service with The Department of Technology Services. Additionally, she worked for The Employment Development Department, The Employment Training Panel, and The Department of General Services. She was also "on-loan" to The Governor's Office. Based on her experience, Michelle advises her clients to always be "testing up". This will maximize opportunities for career advancement in State service.

For the past five years she has taught classes, conducted workshops, and participated in regional job fairs explaining "How to Get a Job with the State." Her clients include outplacement firms, schools, and companies facing closure or downsizing. In her consulting business she works with individuals requesting one-on-one evaluations of their education and experience as it relates to the exams they are eligible to take.

Dedication

This book is dedicated to Dr. Gerard Larson, my mentor-professor in college and his loving wife Georgia, a wonderful teacher in her own right. I credit many of my accomplishments to their guidance and absolute belief in my abilities.

Contents

This book is divided into five sections. The first is a paraphrasing of **"The Six Steps"** listed on the California State Personnel Board's home page (www.spb.ca.gov) covering the process of getting a civil service job. I have modified some of the language, bulleted the information, and reformatted it for an easier read.

The second section is titled **"Quick Tips for Finding Exam Bulletins."** This is a short-cut way to locate the types of exams given with just a few clicks of the mouse. It will also cover some sample exam questions and where to locate them on many exam bulletins.

The third section is titled **"What to Do Now That You Have Passed, Scored, and Are 'Reachable'** on the Exam List." It explains how to be pro-active in locating job openings and what you should include in an application package.

The fourth section is titled **"Additional Information You Might Need."** This contains more tips to help you succeed in landing a State civil service position.

The fifth section is an **appendix** that contains samples of the forms you will use in the civil service application and testing process. Samples include a common exam bulletin, a job bulletin matching the exam title and the standard state application (STD 678) used for both exams and job openings.

This book was written in 2010 and like all information regarding the civil service process, it is subject to change. Refer to the State Personnel Board's website to monitor any changes.

How to Get a State Job

State civil service jobs are filled by using an exam process open to all regardless of race, color, creed, national origin, ancestry, sex, marital status, disability, religious or political affiliation, age or sexual orientation. California residency is not required, and U.S. citizenship is only required for peace officer jobs.

You can apply for State jobs only when you are "reachable" on an exam list. {Reachable means scoring in the top three positions on the exam} This book is a guide to the 6-Step selection process, which begins with the search for an examination and ends with the completion of probation. Examinations are given both by the State Personnel Board (SPB) and by individual State departments. The examination announcement will tell you who is giving the test and where to apply.

FOLLOW THESE 6 STEPS

STEP I. OBTAINING INFORMATION

How to Find it: Options for locating exam bulletins

- The easiest way to learn what examinations are open for testing is to browse the SPB Web site at: *www.spb.ca.gov*. Click on Browse/ State Jobs. More specific details as to locating all "open exams" will be covered in the next section and a sample of an exam bulletin will be found in the appendix.

- Visit the SPB's Sacramento Service Center to access the Web site, obtain copies of examination announcements, state application forms, and other forms and brochures on the civil service employ- ment process. They are located at 801 Capitol Mall, Sacramento, CA

- Go to your local Employment Development Department (EDD) office. They receive and post announcements for State civil service examina- tions and may also have applications and other brochures available.

Examination Announcements:

When you find an examination you are interested in applying for, print out a copy of the exam announcement (bulletin) and read it carefully for "minimum qualifications". If you feel you meet the qualifications listed in the bulletin, you will be directed to take the exam on-line or to send the standard State application form (STD 678) to the agency giving the exam.

STEP 2. APPLYING FOR AN EXAMINATION

How to Apply:

- The State Examination and/or Employment Application (STD 678) form is generic and is used for both exam applications as well as job applications. This form is available from SPB and EDD or can be downloaded from the SPB's Web site. Read it over carefully and answer all questions that apply to you. Your cooperation in answering the questions on the last page is greatly appreciated. Type or print it neatly in ink. The completed application is an example of your reading comprehension skills, your ability to follow directions, and your attention to detail. You should make a copy for yourself in case you need to refer to it later. The bulletin will tell you where to send your application, or if you must apply in person, as well as the last date to apply. The postmark on the envelope is generally used to determine whether you meet the final filing deadline.

Late applications are not accepted.

Application Review:

- If you do not meet the minimum requirements, you will receive a letter within two weeks after the final filing date. You have one week (7days from the date of the letter) to supply additional information that will be reviewed and may render you eligible to take the exam. The agency will then notify you of the exam location and date and what you will need to bring to the exam. If you have not received your acknowledgment one month after the final filing date, you should contact the department conducting the examination to make certain your application was received and that you have been accepted to take the exam when scheduled.

STEP 3. PREPARING FOR THE EXAMINATION

- Go back to the examination announcement and read the section Entitled "Examination Information." It will tell you what type of test will be used and what effect (known as "weight") each test will have on your final score. There are several combinations and variations.

Any one or a combination of the types of tests described here may be used. Read the "Scope" section carefully; it will tell you what subjects will be covered.

If you have a physical disability that may require accommodation in the testing process, you should also obtain a copy of "Important Information for Persons with Disabilities Applying for State Civil Service Examinations" (SPB-83). Written tests are given in a wide variety of locations throughout California. Performance tests and oral tests are usually given only in large metropolitan areas. Candidates are not reimbursed for travel to and from test sites.

Written Test: The test date is printed on the examination announcement. These tests typically consist of multiple-choice questions. Refer to the "Scope of Written Test" on the bulletin to determine what will be on the test. Six to eight weeks after the test, you will receive a notice telling you whether or not you have passed. You will not receive a percentage score until all parts of the examination process are completed. If the written test is pass/fail only, scores are not assigned.

Oral Test/Interview:

- The oral test may be called "Qualifications Appraisal", "Employee Development Appraisal", or "Promotional Readiness Examination". Before going to the interview, review the "Position", "Examination Information", and "Scope" sections of the examination bulletin. In your interview, you may be asked to tell the panel of two to three people about your education and experience and how they have prepared you for this job. The panel will have reviewed your application before you come into the oral interview, and may ask you some situational questions and for more detail on your qualifications. It is in the oral test/interview that you must demonstrate your qualifications to the panel, which will rate you competitively.

Internet/Automated Examination:

- Examinations for some jobs require applicants to apply via the Internet, complete an on-line education and experience examination process, and/or appear at a test site to take a computer-based test. Information regarding these types of examinations can be accessed from the SPB's Internet site at: *www.spb.ca.gov.*

Performance Test:

- Clerical and trades classifications frequently have performance tests in which candidates demonstrate their knowledge of tools and materials or their ability to operate machines or equipment.

Supplemental Application/Achievement Rating Test:

- Consists of essay questions that are mailed out to candidates to be returned before the oral test/interview. They are used as an elaboration of your education and experience and provide information for the interview panel.

Education and Experience Evaluation:

- If the examination announcement states that there may be an Education and Experience Evaluation, it is absolutely critical that you fill out your application as completely and thoroughly as possible. Your score in this type of examination will depend entirely upon the information submitted on your application.

Agility/Physical Ability:

- For law enforcement and some other jobs, physical ability tests are commonly given and are frequently combined with vision and hearing tests. These are usually given just prior to hiring.

STEP 4. EMPLOYMENT LIST

- The names of people that pass all parts of the examination are placed on an employment list. When there are job openings in State civil service, the people scoring in the top three slots (there may be a few or hundreds) on the list are contacted first. The department has the discretion to hire anyone that is certified and eligible on the employment list as long as they are "reachable."

STEP 5. HIRING INTERVIEW

- The oral test you may have taken as part of the examination process was to determine your qualifications for the classification. The hiring interview is specific to a particular job, in a department that uses the classification.

- A classification can be utilized in a wide variety of departments; So, before you go to your job interview, you should acquaint yourself with the mission and functions of that department and know how the job you are interviewing for contributes.

STEP 6. PROBATION

- When you have been hired, you will serve a probationary period of six months to one year. You will receive three probationary reports by your immediate supervisor, which will be discussed with you and reviewed by another supervisor. When you have successfully completed your probation, you will attain permanent status as a State employee.

OTHER IMPORTANT INFORMATION

Career Credits may be granted to eligible State employees in some open examinations.

If Career Credits will be granted, the examination announcement will state it is a "Non- promotional" examination. Three points are added to the final score, but only after the candidate has successfully passed all parts of the examination.

Change of Address: If you move during the examination process or while you are on any employment list, write immediately to the department conducting the examination. It is your responsibility to update your information.

Test Results: It may take up to four weeks to score each part of the examination and to notify all candidates of their results. If you do not receive results within eight weeks of taking any test, contact the department conducting the examination. It is every applicant's responsibility to maintain a copy of his/her final test-results letter. It contains information, such as the title of the examination, the testing department, and your Candidate ID Number. This information is needed if you wish to update/change your personal and list eligibility information.

Veteran's Preference Credits: These are awarded in and open non-promotional entrance examinations requiring less than college graduation AND two years of experience. In OPEN examinations, eligible veterans, widows/widowers of veterans, and spouses of 100% disabled veterans receive 10 points. Eligible disabled veterans receive 15 points. In OPEN NONPROMOTIONAL examinations, eligible veterans receive 5 points. Eligible disabled veterans receive 10 points. Individuals who receive veteran's points are not eligible for career credits pursuant to Sections 18950.1, 18951, and 18951.5.

NOTE: NO PREFERANCE CREDITS FOR VETERANS WILL BE ALLOWED ONCE A VETERAN ACHIEVES PERMANENT CIVIL SERVICE STATUS.
The examination announcement will tell you whether or not Veterans Preference Credits will be awarded. Veterans Points are added to the final score, only after the candidate has successfully passed all parts of the examination. To apply, obtain an "Application for Veterans Preference Form" (SPB-1093) from any departmental testing office and return it with your examination application.

Employment Contacts:

Generally only individuals in reachable ranks (highest three scores) on the employment list, are contacted to apply for vacancies. Due to a number of factors, your ranking on the employment list can change frequently. You may obtain point-in-time information regarding your ranking on the overall employment list using the eligible list disclosure feature on the SPB Web Site. This information is accessible at: *www.spb. ca.gov/employment/eligible_list_disclosure.htm*. Although you are not obligated to interview for every job or to accept the first job that is offered, you are required to respond to all employment contacts. If you waive a total of three contacts or job offers, your name will be removed from the open employment list. Whenever you receive a contact letter (Standard Clearance and Waiver Form), it is imperative that you respond, even if you do not wish to be interviewed. If you fail to respond, it may be assumed that you are no longer interested in being hired from that list, and your name will be made inactive. To be made active again, you must write to the department that conducted the examination.

Proof of Minimum Qualifications:

Some examinations require individuals to self-certify possession of the stated minimum qualifications when they apply to take the examination. Upon request, it is the applicant's responsibility to provide proof of these minimum qualifications to the requesting state department and/ or prior to being eligible for hire. These may include providing copies of official college transcripts, or a typing certificate that verifies the ability to type 40 words per minute. Your name may be withheld or removed permanently from the eligible list if you fail to provide this information or are found not to possess the required minimum qualifications.

Cheating:

A candidate who cheats on any part of a civil service examination may be disqualified from competing in the rest of the examination, removed from other employment lists on which he or she already has eligibility, barred from participating in future examinations, and/or subject to criminal charges.

CONTACT INFORMATION
STATE PERSONNEL BOARD
801 CAPITOL MALL
SACRAMENTO, CA 95814
1-(866)-844-8671
(For callers outside the 916 area code)
TTY* (916) 651-8782
*TTY is a Telecommunications Device for the Deaf and is reachable only from phones equipped with such a device.

QUICK TIPS FOR FINDING EXAM BULLETINS

**Four clicks of the mouse
will take you to all open Exams**

**Remember, you must take, pass,
and place in order to apply
for a civil service job with the state.**

- Log on to the California State Personnel Board's home page @ www. spb.ca.gov

- Click on State Jobs which will take you to the next page.

- Scroll down until you see Browse Job Recruitments and Vacancies and click on > Posted this Past Month

- On the following page click on the shaded cell that says "show all" and wait for that information to load. This will give you all exams in alphabetical order including the ones posted prior to the last month. **Many exams can be taken on the internet and are given on a continuous basis.**

- Once you have reviewed the exams listed in "show all" you can see the new exams being posted on a weekly basis by clicking on "Posted this Past Week" as you continue to monitor exams being offered.

What to do when you find an exam bulletin that interests you:

The most common types of exams: Agency and Internet

When you locate an exam that interests you, click on the title and open the bulletin. The bulletin will give you the following information: Where to send your application (form STD 678) if it's an exam being given by an agency, the date it must be postmarked if it is being sent to the testing agency, and the "Minimum Qualifications" necessary to qualify for you to take the exam. Pay close attention to the minimum qualifications listed because that is the key to your eligibility for taking the exam. Your education and experience must mimic those qualifications in order for you to take the test. Consider all your experience including volunteer work when assessing your education and employment history. Many people tend to discredit experience if they did not get a paycheck for doing it, but experience is experience, work is work, paid or unpaid.

If the exam bulletin says the test is being given on the internet, you must create your Application–on-Line prior to taking the test or tests being offered. You will find this Application-on-Line listed as the first entry under the open exams banner when looking for all exams. After you have completed this application that includes a password, you are free to take the internet exams. Many, but not all exam bulletins will have a sentence that says "Click here to review the Qualifications Assessment Questions". This equates to an open-book exam. Be sure and review these questions and think about your answers before you take the test on-line. There will be a mouse pad graphic at the end of the bulletin prompting you to log on and take the test. Not all internet exams are available all the time even though that is implied in the bulletin. Continue to monitor the exams as they will resume testing at periodic intervals. Most people, including those with little or no education past high school, are eligible to take several exams using their work experience. There are some exams that do not require a high school diploma.

What are the exams like and how can I improve my odds when taking them:

Most state exams are a combination of education and experience evaluations or assessments. As mentioned, if it is an internet exam and you can review the questions that will be asked prior to taking the exam, do so. An example of this option can be found in the bulletin for the Associate Governmental Program Analyst (AGPA) exam. I have copied some of the reviewable questions below:

ASSOCIATE GOVERNMENTAL PROGRAM ANALYST

Using the rating scales provided below, you will self-rate your experience in performing specific job-related tasks and the level at which they were performed.

Respond to each of the following statements by indicating how the statement applies to you. You are required to respond to every statement by marking one option for both of the two scales provided.

In responding to each statement, you may refer to your FORMAL EDUCATION, FORMAL TRAINING COURSES OR WORK EXPERIENCE whether paid or volunteer.

Total Length of Experience:

- More than 3 years experience performing this task
- Over 2 years to 3 years experience performing this task
- Over 1 year to 2 years experience performing this task
- Over 6 months to 1 year experience performing this task
- 0 to 6 months experience performing this task

Level at which the task was performed:

- Performed task as an expert or trained others on task
- Worked independently on task
- Worked under direction on or assisted others with task
- Not performed

QUALIFICATIONS ASSESSMENT

1. Facilitating meetings with groups and teams to coordinate and meet project, program, or organizational objectives.

2. Collaborating with customers or clients to provide service and meet service expectations.

3. Directing and guiding customers and stakeholders on various processes to provide information and/or resolve issues.

4. Addressing problems or customer complaints

   There are many more questions on this exam, but this gives you a preview of how many state exams are worded and the multiple choice options you are given.

If it is an agency exam where you will have to go to the agency's testing location, you should review the "scope of the knowledge" required for the position and reflect on how your skill-sets and education fits those requirements. This information is listed on the exam bulletin. You should also visit the agency's home page and read what the agency is required to do for the state. Reviewing the agency's mission statement, divisions, and overall services will give you a better idea of the agency's purpose.

Some exams are qualification appraisal interviews. This means you will be asked a series of questions by two to three panel members regarding your level of expertise in certain areas as well as the length of time you have performed at that level.

Other exams will be a combination of both written and oral questions. Your combined answers will indicate your score for the exam. Most exams require 70% to pass, but generally speaking, you will have to score much higher in order to be "reachable" (top three rungs) on the exam list. Only successful candidates that score in the top three ranks or rungs of the list are eligible to apply for openings. There may be hundreds or thousands of candidates in the top three rungs on the same exam list. Some will have scores exceeding 100% because they were awarded veterans preference points after they successfully passed the exam. Veteran's points can't be used to help you pass if you did not score a 70%.

WHAT TO DO NOW THAT YOU PASSED, SCORED, AND ARE "REACHABLE":

Although some agencies have the resources to contact successful candidates regarding openings in their various departments, the truth is, you must be **pro-active** in finding openings and applying for them on your own. You might get several "contact" or "inquiry" notices asking if you want to apply for a position. If so, great! Send them an application and follow the instructions on the "inquiry." But the pro-active way requires you to search regularly for any and all openings that match your exam results. To find the openings, you need to drill down on the State Personnel Board's Home page. Go to www.spb.ca.gov. Click on Browse, Jobs, State Jobs. When you get to the next page you will see a sub-title under Job Vacancy Listings >>Vacancy Search (VPOS). Click on that link which will take you to a page with boxes indicating the type of search you want to do. I advise starting with "Easy Search." After opening that page, you should type in one of the significant words (analyst) in the title of the exam you successfully took in the box provided. Leave the "anytime openings" already marked on that page, then click "search." When you are looking regularly you can refine your search to "posted in the past 7 days" to locate new job openings. Once you type in your exam title word, any openings with that title (and others with similar titles) will materialize. It is important to remember that you are only eligible to apply for the exact title of the job matching the title of the exam you took, passed, and placed in the "reachable" range. If you are reachable on the Associate Governmental Program Analyst (AGPA) exam list, that does not render you eligible to apply for a similarly titled job opening like an Associate Governmental Program Analyst (Specialist). It is apples to apples, and oranges to oranges. When you find all the AGPA job openings, open each one individually and read the job bulletin. It contains information on that job as well as the contact person for that opening and where to mail the application. When applying for a position, read what kind of person they are looking for and the job skills that person should posses. I recommend including four basic things in an application package. They are: the STD 678 filled out carefully and completely, a functional resume, (on quality bond paper), a print-out of your exam results unless you're directed to list that on line 12 of the application's first page, and a well written cover letter that highlights why your experience so closely matches the job description. The cover letter gives you the opportunity to customize your application package and include some things not listed on your resume but important for the specific job opening. A cover letter is rarely required but I think it gives you another chance to showcase some writing skills and looks more professional.

Look at the cut-off date for submitting the application (though many will say "until filled") and make certain you get it to them on time. It often takes more than two or three weeks for a response due to the number of applications the agency receives. Some will send you a letter saying they selected others for an interview. Sometimes you will hear nothing at all because there wasn't anyone available to respond to the sheer volume of applications received. Don't despair and don't take it personally. This is a numbers game. The more exams you take, pass, and score in the "reachable" range, the more opportunities you have to apply for multiple job openings. It is not uncommon for someone to have taken and be eligible on entry level lists such at Office Technician (Typing) as well as the Associate Governmental Analyst list. The important thing is to get in wherever the opportunity presents itself. You can apply for other openings within the state as they materialize in VPOS. Many people start as an Office Technician and within a year they have moved on to a higher paying job that more closely matches their experience and educational background. Generally speaking, California allows you time off to interview for other state positions without using your vacation time or docking your pay while you are interviewing.

ADDITIONAL TIPS YOU NEED TO KNOW

1. Take as many exams (both internet and agency) as you are qualified to take. Apply for agency exams even though they might not be given for months after you submit your STD 678 application. Remember, the more exams you pass and are listed as "reachable" the more job opportunities you will have. Think of a dart board. The more darts you throw (tests you take) and the more bulls eyes you hit (reachable range on the list) the greater the odds of landing an interview and a state job.

2. Take note of when you placed on an exam list as most expire after 12 months. If you do not score in the top three ranks, take the exam again when you can and keep taking it until you score in the reachable range. You must take the exam again and score in the "reachable" range in order to continue to apply for openings with that title. Many exams make you wait 12 months before you can retest, but others like the AGPA can be taken again after 6 months.

3. Two of the most common entry level exams are Office Technician (Typing) or Office Technician (General). Two of the most common analyst positions are Staff Services Analyst and Associate Governmental Program Analyst. These classifications are used by multiple state agencies and testing successfully gives you more employment opportunities. A sample of the Associate Governmental Program Analyst (AGPA) exam and a job bulletin matching that title are located in the appendix of this book.

4. It can take from six months to two years to be hired by the state. The process of testing and applying for job openings can be time consuming. Remember, it is imperative that you continue to test for all the exams you are eligible to take being offered at any given time. It can be very frustrating to go through this tedious process but the sooner you start, the closer you will be to job opportunities. My successful clients are the ones who do not give up. In real estate we know its location, location, location. In getting hired by the state it is tenacity, tenacity, tenacity!

5. After you are working for the state, continue to test for the next promotional opportunity. When you are a state employee, you will be given additional opportunities to take "promotional exams." Sometimes these exams are given by your agency, other times by different agencies. These exams are for current state employees only. There is every reason to continue to test-up for better jobs, more career opportunities, and more money.

6. Another issue to consider after you are hired is agency funding. Agencies which have more stable sources of funding are less likely to be severely impacted when budget cuts come (and they always do). Think of the state as giant family. Some of the relatives (agencies) are richer than others because they collect fees and are not dependent solely on the "general fund" for hiring or lay-offs.

7. If you suffer from a disability that prevents you from working full-time but can work part time, review the state's program for "LEAP" eligibility found on the State Personnel Board's Home page. Follow the steps for LEAP certification and test for all the exams reserved for persons with that classification. You are entitled to full benefits even if you work only part time which is usually 20 hours per week but can be flexible based on the agency and your situation.

8. If you are a veteran, please read the information found under Veteran's Information listed on the SPB Home page. You are often entitled to extra points that will be added to you test scores after

you successfully pass a state exam. Widows of veterans are eligible for points in some instances as well.

9. People who are not citizens of the United States but have legal residence are eligible to work for the state in almost all agencies.

10. To reiterate, getting a job with the state can take months to years. That's because it's a "process" and involves taking exams, placing in the reachable rank, finding openings that correlate to that exam title, and finally being the successful applicant for that opening. Do not give up! Like all things it takes time, patience, and perseverance. The reward is securing one of the more stable career paths in today's ever changing world. While there are no guarantees in life, civil service has proven to be one of the more viable options for long-term employment.

11. Finally, the "Baby Boomers" are retiring in record numbers. Despite the constant budget crisis faced by most state governments, they can only cut back so much. There are over 200,000 state employees in California, a state with close to 40 million residents. The odds favor a constant opportunity for civil service employment.

APPENDIX

The following samples included are the **most common forms** of information you will use in testing and applying for jobs. These materials were copied from the State Personnel Board's website and reformatted to fit this book. They are not legible but it will give the reader a visual reference when looking for them on-line. The information will change periodically but it gives you some idea of what was referenced in the text of this book. I am not including the LEAP certification forms or the Veterans preference point forms. These forms can be found easily and printed out using the www.spb.ca.gov website.

Most Common Forms

1. The Standard State Application (STD678). This document is used for both exams given by agencies as well as job openings.

2. An exam bulletin for the ASSOCIATE GOVERNMENTAL PROGRAM ANLAYST (AGPA). This exam is given on-line.

3. A sample job bulletin for AGPA.

How to Get a State Job

STATE OF CALIFORNIA - STATE PERSONNEL BOARD
EXAMINATION AND/OR EMPLOYMENT APPLICATION
STD. 678 (REV. 8/2009) Page 6

INSTRUCTIONS

Read the following instructions carefully before completing this Application. Please complete the Application on a typewriter or personal computer or print in ink. All questions **must** be answered completely and accurately, except as noted. You may be disqualified for any false or misleading statements or for omitting information. The information you furnish will be used to determine your eligibility and/or may be the basis for arriving at your final rating in an examination. During the course of an examination, you may be requested to provide additional information regarding your qualifications, your preference regarding work location, shifts, etc.

Easy ID - You are required to provide the following tracking information on the application. The first three letters of your last name at birth, the month and day of your birth and the last four digits of your social security number. If you have already established an Easy ID in the online system and it is different, please provide that Easy ID.

Social Security Number - Providing this is voluntary in accordance with the Privacy Act of 1974 (PS 93-579). However, if the Social Security Number is not provided, the department administering this examination will be unable to process your application for purposes of granting Veteran's Preference points, Career Credits, written test waivers, or to check for eligibility in promotional examinations.

Home/VRS/TTY Number - Provide your 10-digit home telephone, Video Relay Service (VRS) phone number, or Text Telephone (TTY) phone number.

Examination Title/Job Title - Fill in the exact title of the examination from the examination bulletin. Only civil service employees who meet the definition of a promotional candidate may file for promotional examinations. All others must file for open examinations. If applying for a vacant position, enter the class title of the position for which you are applying.

Question 2 - Reasonable Accommodation will be provided to applicants who need assistance to take an interview or written test. If you check "Yes" you will be contacted via telephone or mail to make specific arrangements.

Question 5 - Employment History/Discharges. Question 5 must be answered by all applicants. You must answer "Yes" if you have ever, because of poor performance or misconduct, been fired, dismissed, or terminated from a job, or had an employment contract terminated. Explain any "Yes" answers in Item 12. Include the facts in brief, the grounds for any action taken against you, and the circumstances under which you left the position.

In completing this application, you do not need to answer "Yes" to Question 5 if:

- you have been rejected during a probationary period; or
- your employer withdrew the firing, dismissal, termination, or contract termination (either voluntarily or as part of a settlement); or
- a court or administrative agency overturned or revoked the firing, dismissal, termination, or contract termination.

If asked about past employment history by a prospective employer during the hiring process or probationary period, however, applicants are required to tell the truth regarding any firing, dismissal, termination, contract termination or rejection during probationary period, whether or not the action was overturned, revoked, or withdrawn (either voluntarily by the employer or, as part of a settlement agreement). Applicants are also required to provide factually correct information on the "Employment History" section of the application (Item No. 15).

Questions 8 through 11 - These questions should be answered only if the examination bulletin indicates (a) a minimum or maximum age requirement for eligibility; (b) a California Driver License requirement; or (c) the examination is for a peace officer classification. You should review the examination bulletin carefully for details and the circumstances under which you may answer "No" to Items 10 or 11.

12. Explanations - Use this space to explain the details of any response that requires additional information. Be thorough, and attach additional sheet(s) if needed.

Signature - Your signature and the date signed is required. If the Application is not signed, it may be rejected.

13. Education - You must include a complete record of your training and educational background. Please read the Requirements section of the examination bulletin carefully for any special educational requirements. If more space is needed, attach additional sheet(s).

14. Licenses - If the examination bulletin calls for a specific license, professional certificate, or membership in a professional organization, list the full name of the license, certificate or organization, the license number, and the official expiration date of the document or membership.

15. Experience - You must include a complete list of your paid and/or volunteer work experience **which relates to the qualification requirements specified on the examination bulletin.** List all relevant jobs, during the past 10 years, regardless of duration, including part-time and military service. You should also list volunteer experience and jobs held more than ten years ago if they relate directly to the job for which you are applying. **State employees must list the specific departments for which they worked and indicate the specific civil service class title(s) held.**

If Veteran's Preference Points - are being granted in this examination and you qualify, you must apply for the points on Application for Veteran's Preference Form SPB-1093.

NOTE: Your completed Application and other examination related information submitted to the department administering this examination becomes confidential information and the property of the State of California as provided by Government Code Section 18934. This Application and other confidential information **will not be returned;** therefore, we recommend that you keep a copy of your completed Application for your personal records. Your rights to inspect your examination papers are set forth in Sections 186-189 of Title 2 of the California Code of Regulations, which can be accessed on the State Personnel Board's website at **www.spb.ca.gov.**

PLEASE ENTER YOUR NAME ON PAGES 1 THROUGH 4 AND STAPLE ALL PAGES OF THE APPLICATION TOGETHER BEFORE SUBMITTING!

APPENDIX

**EXAMINATION AND/OR
EMPLOYMENT APPLICATION**

Applications will be processed ONLY for classifications where an examination is in progress and the published final filing date has not passed, or for vacant positions where a department requests an application.

STD. 678 (REV. 8/2009) Page 1

PRINT OR TYPE — PLEASE SEE INSTRUCTIONS ON BACK PAGE

APPLICANT IDENTIFICATION NUMBER (EASY ID) FIRST 3 LETTERS OF LAST NAME AT BIRTH	MONTH OF BIRTH	DAY OF BIRTH	LAST 4 DIGITS OF SOCIAL SECURITY NUMBER

APPLICANT'S NAME *(Last)*   *(First)*   *(M.I.)*   SOCIAL SECURITY NUMBER

MAILING ADDRESS *(Number)*   *(Street)*   E-MAIL ADDRESS   WORK TELEPHONE NUMBER

(City)   *(County)*   *(State)*   *(Zip Code)*   HOME/VRS/TTY TELEPHONE NUMBER

EXAMINATION(S) OR JOB TITLE(S) FOR WHICH YOU ARE APPLYING   PERSONNEL USE ONLY

FOR SPOT EXAMINATIONS, ENTER THE LOCATION WHERE YOU WISH TO WORK

ANSWER THE FOLLOWING QUESTIONS: (Answer questions 8, 9, 10, and/or 11 only if the examination indicates they are required.)

1. Enter the county in which you would like to take the examination if different from the county of your residence: _____

2. Do you need reasonable accommodation to take an interview or written test? _____ ☐ YES ☐ NO

3. Do your religious beliefs prevent you from taking an examination on Saturday? _____ ☐ YES ☐ NO

4. Are you now employed by the State of California? (If "YES", fill in the information below.) _____ ☐ YES ☐ NO
   Department: _____ Subdivision: _____

5. Have you ever been fired, dismissed, terminated, or had an employment contract terminated from any position for performance or for disciplinary reasons? (Applicants who have been rejected during a probationary period, or whose dismissals or terminations have been overturned, withdrawn [unilaterally or as part of a settlement agreement] or revoked need not answer "Yes".) Refer to the Instructions for further information. If "Yes" to Question #5, give details in Item #12.   ☐ YES ☐ NO

6. In addition to English, list any other languages you:
   a. possess verbal fluency in _____
   b. possess written fluency in _____

7. I certify I can type at a speed of _____ words per minute. (For typing applicants only.)

(Answer Questions 8, 9, 10, and/or 11 ONLY if the examination indicates they are required.)

8. Do you meet the minimum and/or maximum age requirements? _____ ☐ YES ☐ NO

9. Do you possess a valid California Driver License? (If "YES", fill in the information below.) _____ ☐ YES ☐ NO
   License# _____ Class: _____ Restrictions: _____

10. Have you ever been convicted by any court of a misdemeanor crime of domestic violence? _____ ☐ YES ☐ NO

11. Have you ever been convicted by any court of a felony? _____ ☐ YES ☐ NO

12. EXPLANATIONS

CERTIFICATION – IMPORTANT – PLEASE READ BEFORE SIGNING – If not signed, this application may be rejected.

I certify under penalty of perjury that the information I have entered on this application is true and complete to the best of my knowledge. I further understand that any false, incomplete, or incorrect statements may result in my disqualification from the examination process or dismissal from employment with the State of California. I authorize the employers and educational institutions identified on this application to release any information they may have concerning my employment or education to the State of California.

APPLICANT'S SIGNATURE   DATE SIGNED

APPLICANTS—DO NOT USE THE SPACE BELOW—FOR PERSONNEL USE ONLY

Classes	01	02	03	04	05	06		FOR PERSONNEL USE ONLY	
WC for Series/Levels							Flags — — — — — — —	STATUS	
RC/Flag for Series/Levels							WC —	☐ ACCEPTED ☐ REJECTED WC___	
								EXPERIENCE	LICENSE REQUIREMENT
CODES								EDUCATION	OTHER
								STAFF	DATE PROCESSED

How to Get a State Job

EXAMINATION AND/OR
EMPLOYMENT APPLICATION

STD. 678 (REV. 8/2009) Page 2

APPLICANT'S NAME (Last)	(First)	(M.I.)	SOCIAL SECURITY NUMBER

13. EDUCATION

DID YOU GRADUATE FROM HIGH SCHOOL?   IF NOT, DO YOU POSSESS A GED OR EQUIVALENT?   IF NOT, ENTER THE HIGHEST GRADE YOU COMPLETED

☐ YES   ☐ NO   ☐ YES   ☐ NO

UNIVERSITY OR COLLEGE—NAME AND LOCATION, BUSINESS, CORRESPONDENCE, TRADE OR SERVICE SCHOOL	COURSE OF STUDY	UNITS COMPLETED		DIPLOMA, DEGREE OR CERTIFICATE OBTAINED	DATE COMPLETED
		SEMESTER	QUARTER		

14. LIST BELOW VALID LICENSES, CERTIFICATES OF PROFESSIONAL OR VOCATIONAL COMPETENCE, OR MEMBERSHIP IN PROFESSIONAL ASSOCIATIONS CALLED FOR IN THIS EXAMINATION ANNOUNCEMENT. *(If you are an attorney, please include first Bar date with license information if the examination announcement requires it.)*

LICENSE/CERTIFICATION NUMBER	DATE ADMITTED TO THE BAR	EXPIRATION DATE	IN THE SPACE BELOW, INDICATE SPECIFIC COURSE REQUIREMENTS NEEDED TO SATISFY REQUIREMENTS FOR THIS EXAMINATION

15. EMPLOYMENT HISTORY– *Begin with your most recent job. List each job separately.*

FROM (M/D/Y)	TO (M/D/Y)	TITLE/JOB CLASSIFICATION (Include Range or Level, if applicable)	
HOURS PER WEEK	TOTAL WORKED (Years/Months)	COMPANY/STATE AGENCY NAME	SUPERVISOR
SALARY EARNED		ADDRESS	
$ PER			

DUTIES PERFORMED

REASON FOR LEAVING

FROM (M/D/Y)	TO (M/D/Y)	TITLE/JOB CLASSIFICATION (Include Range or Level, if applicable)	
HOURS PER WEEK	TOTAL WORKED (Years/Months)	COMPANY/STATE AGENCY NAME	SUPERVISOR
SALARY EARNED		ADDRESS	
$ PER			

DUTIES PERFORMED

REASON FOR LEAVING

APPENDIX

STATE OF CALIFORNIA — STATE PERSONNEL BOARD

**EXAMINATION AND/OR
EMPLOYMENT APPLICATION**

STD. 678 (REV. 8/2009)   Page 3

APPLICANT'S NAME *(Last)*	*(First)*	*(M.I.)*	SOCIAL SECURITY NUMBER

15. EMPLOYMENT HISTORY *(Continued)*

FROM *(M/D/Y)*	TO *(M/D/Y)*	TITLE/JOB CLASSIFICATION *(Include Range or Level, if applicable)*	
HOURS PER WEEK	TOTAL WORKED (Years/Months)	COMPANY/STATE AGENCY NAME	SUPERVISOR
SALARY EARNED		ADDRESS	
$ PER			

DUTIES PERFORMED

REASON FOR LEAVING

FROM *(M/D/Y)*	TO *(M/D/Y)*	TITLE/JOB CLASSIFICATION *(Include Range or Level, if applicable)*	
HOURS PER WEEK	TOTAL WORKED (Years/Months)	COMPANY/STATE AGENCY NAME	SUPERVISOR
SALARY EARNED		ADDRESS	
$ PER			

DUTIES PERFORMED

REASON FOR LEAVING

FROM *(M/D/Y)*	TO *(M/D/Y)*	TITLE/JOB CLASSIFICATION *(Include Range or Level, if applicable)*	
HOURS PER WEEK	TOTAL WORKED (Years/Months)	COMPANY/STATE AGENCY NAME	SUPERVISOR
SALARY EARNED		ADDRESS	
$ PER			

DUTIES PERFORMED

REASON FOR LEAVING

STATE OF CALIFORNIA — STATE PERSONNEL BOARD

**EXAMINATION AND/OR
EMPLOYMENT APPLICATION**

STD. 678 (REV. 8/2009) Page 4

APPLICANT'S NAME *(Last)*	*(First)*	*(M.I.)*	SOCIAL SECURITY NUMBER

---

15. EMPLOYMENT HISTORY *(Continued)*

FROM *(M/D/Y)*	TO *(M/D/Y)*	TITLE/JOB CLASSIFICATION *(Include Range or Level, if applicable)*	
HOURS PER WEEK	TOTAL WORKED *(Years/Months)*	COMPANY/STATE AGENCY NAME	SUPERVISOR
SALARY EARNED		ADDRESS	
$	PER		

DUTIES PERFORMED

REASON FOR LEAVING

FROM *(M/D/Y)*	TO *(M/D/Y)*	TITLE/JOB CLASSIFICATION *(Include Range or Level, if applicable)*	
HOURS PER WEEK	TOTAL WORKED *(Years/Months)*	COMPANY/STATE AGENCY NAME	SUPERVISOR
SALARY EARNED		ADDRESS	
$	PER		

DUTIES PERFORMED

REASON FOR LEAVING

FROM *(M/D/Y)*	TO *(M/D/Y)*	TITLE/JOB CLASSIFICATION *(Include Range or Level, if applicable)*	
HOURS PER WEEK	TOTAL WORKED *(Years/Months)*	COMPANY/STATE AGENCY NAME	SUPERVISOR
SALARY EARNED		ADDRESS	
$	PER		

DUTIES PERFORMED

REASON FOR LEAVING

APPENDIX

STATE OF CALIFORNIA — STATE PERSONNEL BOARD

**EXAMINATION AND/OR
EMPLOYMENT APPLICATION**

STD. 678 (REV. 8/2009) Page 5

EQUAL EMPLOYMENT OPPORTUNITY
(For Examination Use Only)

APPLICANT: To assist the State of California in its commitment to Equal Employment Opportunity, applicants are asked to voluntarily provide the following information. This questionnaire will be separated from the application prior to the examination and will not be used in any employment decisions. Government Code Section 19705 authorizes the State Personnel Board to retain this information for research and statistical purposes.

APPLICANT IDENTIFICATION NUMBER

| FIRST 3 LETTERS OF LAST NAME AT BIRTH | | MONTH OF BIRTH | | DAY OF BIRTH | | LAST 4 DIGITS OF SOCIAL SECURITY NUMBER | |

AGE

☐ (1) UNDER 21   ☐ (3) 21 - 39   ☐ (6) 40 - 69   ☐ (7) 70 AND OVER

GENDER

☐ MALE   ☐ FEMALE

Ethnic Category *(Please check the box that best describes your race/ethnicity.)*:

☐ (7) **AMERICAN INDIAN OR ALASKAN NATIVE**—Persons having origins in any of the tribal peoples of North America, and who maintain cultural identification through tribal affiliation or community recognition.

ENTER TRIBAL IDENTIFICATION OR AFFILIATION

☐ (2) **ASIAN**—Persons having origins in any of the original peoples of the Far East, Southeast Asia, or the Indian Subcontinent. This includes China, Japan, and Korea.

☐ (1) **BLACK**—Persons having origins in any of the black racial groups of Africa.

☐ (8) **FILIPINO**—Persons having origins in any of the original peoples of the Philippine Islands.

☐ (4) **HISPANIC**—Persons of Mexican, Puerto Rican, Cuban, Central or South American, or other Spanish culture or origin, regardless of race.

☐ (6) **PACIFIC ISLANDERS**—Persons having origins in the Pacific Islands, such as Samoa.

☐ (5) **WHITE**—Persons having origins in any of the original peoples of Europe, North Africa, or the Middle East.

Check if:

☐ (3) **OTHER** *(Specify)* _____

☐ (Y) **DISABLED**—A person with a disability is an individual who: (1) has a physical or mental impairment or medical condition that limits one or more life activities, such as walking, speaking, breathing, performing manual tasks, seeing, hearing, learning, caring for oneself or working; (2) has a record or history of such impairment or medical condition; or (3) is regarded as having such an impairment or medical condition.

☐ **MILITARY**—A military veteran; a widow or widower of a veteran; or a spouse of a 100% disabled veteran.

How did you learn of this Examination?

☐ TELEPHONE JOB LINE   ☐ WORD OF MOUTH   ☐ INTERNET

☐ ADVERTISEMENT IN _____   ☐ EXAMINATION BULLETIN LOCATED AT _____

THANK YOU FOR COMPLETING THIS QUESTIONNAIRE

How to Get a State Job

SPB   Home   Find Recruitments   How to Apply   Why Work for CA   My Profile   Español

Search Job Recruitments   Transfer and Reinstatement   Notify Me of New Recruitments   Closed and Ongoing Recruitments Status Board   FAQ

Home   Jobs   **Job Recruitment Bulletin**

Powered by Job…

Associate Governmental Program Analyst
(MULTI-DEPARTMENTAL OPEN)
Recruitment #097500-00105393-9PB04

Department(s):	
	State Personnel Board/Statewide
	State Air Resources Board
	Dept of Rehabilitation
	Dept of General Services
	CA Emergency Management Agency
	Office of Legislative Counsel
	Natural Resources Agency
	Ca Postsecondary Education Commission
	Victim Compensation & Government Claims Board
	Dept of Housing & Community Development
	Dept of Boating & Waterways
	Dept of Food & Agriculture
	Dept of Education
	Dept of Finance
	Dept of Industrial Relations
	Dept of Veterans Affairs
	Department of Motor Vehicles
	Dept of Conservation
	Prison Industry Authority
	Dept of Corrections & Rehabilitation
	Department of Consumer Affairs
	California Housing Finance Agency
	Department of Transportation
	Employment Development Department
	Department of Insurance
	Department of Fish and Game
	Business, Transportation and Housing Agency
	Department of Justice
	Secretary of State
	Board of Equalization
	Department of Water Resources
	California Conservation Corps
	State Energy Resource Conservation and Development Commission
	Department of Corporations
	Public Employees Retirement System
	Franchise Tax Board
	Department of Real Estate
	State Personnel Board
	California Student Aid Commission
	Department of Forestry & Fire Protection
	Commission on Teacher Credentialing
	Fair Political Practices Commission
	Department of Alcoholic Beverage Control
	California Coastal Commission
	State Teachers Retirement System
	San Francisco Bay Conservation & Development Commission
	Department of Alcohol and Drug Programs
	Department of Health Care Services
	Dept of Mental Health
	Department of Social Services
	Department of Developmental Services
	Office of Statewide Health Planning and Development
	State Council On Developmental Disabilities
	Department of Fair Employment & Housing
	Department of Personnel Administration
	Emergency Medical Services Authority

APPENDIX

Commission on Aging
California State Lottery
Department of Community Services and Development
Employment Training Panel
Department of Toxic Substances Control
Department of Pesticide Regulation
Office of Environmental Health Hazard Assessment
Bureau of State Audits
California Earthquake Authority
Office of the Inspector General
Department of Child Support Services
California Workforce Investment Board
Department of Managed Health Care
California Gambling Control Commission
Labor and Workforce Development Agency
Office of Systems Integration
Department of Public Health
Office of The State Chief Information Officer
Delta Stewardship Council
Department of Resources Recycling and Recovery

Opening Date:	9/27/2009 2:00:00 PM
Closing Date:	Continuous
Cut-off Date:	6/14/2014
Type of Recruitment:	Multi-Departmental Open
Salary:	MONTHLY-RANGED-SALARY - $4,400.00 to $5,348.00
Employment Type:	Permanent Full-time
	Permanent Part-time
	Permanent Intermittent
	Limited Term Full-time
	Limited Term Part-Time
	Limited Term Intermittent
Exam Type:	State-wide

Go Back   View Benefits

EEO

An equal opportunity employer to all regardless of race, color, creed, national origin, ancestry, sex, marital status, disability, religious or political affiliation, age or sexual orientation.

DRUG FREE STATEMENT

It is an objective of the state of California to achieve a drug-free state work place. Any applicant for state employment will be expected to behave in accordance with this objective because the use of illegal drugs is inconsistent with the law of the state, the rules governing civil service and the special trust placed in public servants.

WHO SHOULD APPLY?

Candidates who meet the minimum qualifications as stated below may apply for this examination at any time. Once you have taken the examination, you may not reapply for six (6) months. All applicants must meet the education and/or experience requirements as stated on this examination announcement.

FILING INSTRUCTIONS

Final File Date: Continuous

Where to Apply:
Click on the Apply Online link at the bottom of this bulletin.

EMPLOYMENT LIST INFORMATION

An open, merged eligible list will be established by the State Personnel Board for use by other state departments. The names of successful competitors will be merged onto the eligible list in order of final scores regardless of test date. Eligibility expires 12 months after it is established. Once you have taken the Qualifications Assessment, you may not retake it for 6 (six) months.

REQUIREMENTS FOR ADMITTANCE TO THE EXAMINATION

NOTE: All applicants must meet the education and/or experience requirements as stated on this examination announcement.

MINIMUM QUALIFICATIONS

Experience applicable to one of the following patterns may be combined on a proportional basis with experience applicable to the other patterns to meet the

How to Get a State Job

total experience requirements, provided that the combined qualifying experience totals at least 30 months. Education may not be used to reduce this 30-month limit.

Either I

One year of experience performing the duties of a Staff Services Analyst, Range C.

Or II

Experience: Three years of professional analytical experience performing duties in one or a combination of the following or closely related areas: budgeting, management analysis, personnel, planning, program evaluation, or policy analysis. (State experience applied toward this pattern must include at least one year in a class at a level of responsibility equivalent to that of a Staff Services Analyst, Range C.)

and

Education: Equivalent to graduation from college. (Additional qualifying experience may be substituted for the required education on a year-for-year basis.) (One year of graduate work in public or business administration, industrial relations, psychology, law, political science, or a related field may be substituted for six months of the required experience.)

Promotional candidates who are within six months of satisfying the experience requirement for this class will be admitted to the examination, but they must fully meet the experience requirement before being eligible for appointment.

POSITION DESCRIPTION

An Associate Governmental Program Analyst performs the more responsible, varied, and complex technical analytical staff services assignments such as program evaluation and planning; policy analysis and formulation; systems development; budgeting, planning, management, and personnel analysis; and continually provide consultative services to management or others. This is the full journey level analyst class. Incumbents are typically subject-matter generalists who have demonstrated possession of intellectual abilities, the management tools, and the personal qualifications to succeed in a variety of general staff services settings.

Vacancies are anticipated at various departments throughout state service.

EXAMINATION INFORMATION

QUALIFICATIONS ASSESSMENT – Weighted 100.00%

The examination will consist of a Qualifications Assessment and is the sole component of the Associate Governmental Program Analyst examination. To obtain a position on the eligible list, a minimum score of 70% must be received. Competitors will receive his/her score immediately upon completion of the Qualifications Assessment.

Click here to view the Qualifications Assessment questions.

SCOPE:
Knowledge of:

1. Proper spelling, grammar, punctuation, and sentence structure.
2. Data collection techniques.

Ability to:

1. Communicate information clearly and concisely to audiences with varying levels of understanding.
2. Evaluate written materials.
3. Develop procedures and processes related to programs.
4. Review and edit written materials for proper content, format, grammar, punctuation, and sentence structure.
5. Conduct research of various written and electronic materials.
6. Conduct research from various verbal/oral sources.
7. Perform arithmetic computations.
8. Present numerical data in a clear and logical format.
9. Exercise sound judgment when making decisions.
10. Extract specific, relevant data and information from a larger body of material.
11. Read and comprehend various technical documents such as policies, procedures, standards, regulations, technical reports, and contracts.
12. Read and interpret charts and graphs.
13. Reconcile discrepancies in data and information.
14. Identify, analyze, and evaluate situations or problems to determine and implement appropriate courses of action.
15. Apply information through research and/or training to current assignments or projects.
16. Analyze and evaluate the impact and effectiveness of programs, policies, and/or

APPENDIX

procedures.

17. Identify information, data, materials, and resources needed to complete a project or assignment.
18. Introduce change in a positive manner to generate support for the change and minimize the perceived impact on others.
19. Work on multiple tasks or parts of tasks simultaneously to ensure timely completion.
20. Work independently on projects or assignments.
21. Use a personal computer to input data, access information, and/or create materials or documents using a variety of software applications.
22. Use electronic mail software to communicate with diverse audiences.
23. Use database software to input, organize, track, and retrieve data.
24. Use spreadsheet software to compile, compute, organize, and present tables, graphs, and charts.
25. Use the internet to conduct on-line research and obtain information to complete program or project activities, etc.
26. Use word processing software to prepare reports and correspondence.
27. Use and operate basic office equipment.
28. Establish and maintain cooperative working relationships with management, staff, and internal/external stakeholders.
29. Persuade or influence others through the verbal explanation of issues and data.
30. Negotiate and compromise.
31. Use tact and diplomacy.
32. Be flexible in adapting to changes in priorities and assignments.
33. Maintain the confidentiality of sensitive and confidential information obtained through the course of completing assignments.
34. Provide one-on-one training to facilitate the transfer of specific knowledge and/or skills.
35. Interpret data obtained through formal data gathering techniques, such as surveys, questionnaires, and interviews.
36. Develop detailed and specific procedures and processes outlining the steps to follow in completing departmental, program, and/or project tasks.
37. Prioritize and schedule the work to be completed by a work team or project task force.
38. Establish project schedules and milestones to complete projects and assignments within desired timelines.
39. Facilitate meetings and discussions in a manner that ensures that the meeting and discussion stays focused on the intended topic and encourages active participation by all attendees.
40. Function as a liaison on behalf of assigned program or project to interact with management, staff, internal and external stakeholders to provide program specific information, answer questions, and address issues/problems raised.

BENEFITS

- Employer/employee paid health and dental insurance
- Employer paid vision insurance
- Paid Vacation/Sick/Annual Leave Benefits
- 14 paid holidays
- Employer paid disability insurance
- Defined Benefit Retirement Program (upon vesting)
- Employee paid deferred compensation program (401K and 457)
- Flexible work schedules and work hours
- Pre-tax reimbursement for medical care, child care and parking programs
- Employee Assistance Program
- Career development/professional advancement

VETERANS PREFERENCE

Veterans' Preference credits will NOT be granted in the examination as it does not meet the requirements to qualify for Veterans' Preference credit.

CAREER CREDITS

Career Credits will not be added to the final score of this examination.

CONTACT INFORMATION

State Personnel Board
Exam Services Unit
801 Capitol Mall
Sacramento, CA 95814
1-866-844-8671

California Relay (Telephone) Service for the Deaf/Hearing Impaired: From TDD: 1-800-735-2929, From Voice: 1 (800) 735-2922

GENERAL INFORMATION

If you meet the requirements stated on this bulletin, you may take this examination, which is competitive. Possession of the entrance requirement does not assure a place on the eligible list. Your performance in the examination will be compared with the performance of the others who take this test and all candidates who pass will be ranked according to their scores.

How to Get a State Job

The State Personnel Board reserves the right to revise the examination plan to better meet the needs of the service, if the circumstances under which this examination was planned change. Such revision will be in accordance with civil service laws and rules and all competitors will be notified.

Candidates needing special testing arrangements due to a disability must mark the appropriate box on the Standard State Application (STD 678) and/or contact the testing department.

General Qualifications: Candidates must possess essential personal qualifications including integrity, initiative, dependability, good judgment, and ability to work cooperatively with others; and a state of health consistent with the ability to perform the assigned duties of the class. A medical examination may be required. In open examinations, investigation may be made of employment records and personal history and fingerprinting may be required.

Eligible Lists: Eligible lists established by competitive examination, regardless of date, must be used in the following order: 1) subdivisional promotional, 2) departmental promotional, 3) multidepartmental promotional, 4) servicewide promotional, 5) departmental open, 6) open. When there are two lists of the same kind, the older must be used first. Eligible lists will expire in one to four years unless otherwise stated on the bulletin.

High School Equivalence is Required: Equivalence to completion of the 12th grade may be demonstrated in any one of the following ways:1) passing the General Educational Development (GED) Test; 2) completion of 12 semester units of college work; 3) certification from the State Department of Education, a local school board, or high school authorities that the candidate is considered to have education equivalent to graduation from high school; 4) for clerical and accounting classes, substitution of business college work in place of high school on a year-for-year basis. **NOTE: For peace officer classifications, please refer to the testing department for special requirements.**

Click on a link below to apply for this position:

Fill out the Supplemental Questionnaire and Application NOW using the Internet.

Apply Online

Print Personal Preferences Form.

If you did NOT apply online and need to update your location preferences, time-base/ tenure and other preferences, you can print a customized pdf version of the Personal Preference Form. If you did apply online, you can easily update your preferences from your personal status board for each recruitment by logging in to your Personal Status Board.

View and print the Supplemental Questionnaire.

This recruitment requires completion of a supplemental questionnaire. You may view and print the supplemental questionnaire here.

View and print the official application form as an Acrobat pdf file.

A State of California application form is required for this recruitment. You may print this Acrobat PDF document and then fill it in.

Contact us via conventional means.

You may contact us by phone at (866) 844-8671, or e-mail at JobExamCerts@spb.ca.gov, or apply for a job in person at the California State Personnel Board.

You will need Acrobat Reader to download a .pdf file. If you don't have it and want to download the paper application and, if required, supplemental form, click here first Get Acrobat Reader

APPENDIX

Welcome to the
STATE PERSONNEL BOARD

Home Jobs Training Legal Bilingual Services Publications Civil Rights Programs About SPB Español

How to Apply? Benefits Exams Recruiting Resources Vacancy Search (VPOS) FAQ

Home ⟩ Jobs ⟩ VPOS

Vacancy Search (VPOS)

eNotify Me

Enter your email address to be notified when new **ASSOCIATE GOVERNMENTAL PROGRAM ANALYST** vacancies are posted.

COMMUNITY SERVICES & DEVELOPMENT, DEPARTMENT OF

Title: ASSOCIATE GOVERNMENTAL PROGRAM ANALYST
Salary: $4,400.00 - $5,348.00
Posted: 02/09/10

Start A New Search

View in Printer
Friendly Format

Job Description:
The Department of Community Services and Development (CSD)is recruiting to fill a permanent, full time Associate Governmental Program Analyst position. The final filing date is until filled. CSD is 100% federally funded. All applications (Std. 678) must include a Statement of Qualifications that demonstrates your knowledge, experience, skills, education level and other characteristics that make you a great fit for this position. Please identify Bulletin 09-54A and your appointment eligibility (i.e., list, transfer, etc.) in Box 12 of your application. All applicants must have state civil service eligibility. The Department of Community Services and Development (CSD) is the State's leading anti-poverty agency, and administers local community service and energy programs to help low-income Californians achieve self-sufficiency and attain a higher quality of life. CSD is a small department seeking highly-skilled professionals who are committed to the mission, to join the team and partner with our local service providers in an effort to reduce and eliminate poverty. All positions at CSD are 100% federally funded. What Does Working at CSD Offer? Please apply if you appreciate:
•Meaningful work. •Highly interactive teamwork and project-based management. •Opportunities for significant responsibility, creativity and decision-making for self-starters. •Work environment that emphasizes customer service and accountability to local community based organizations, funding sources and the public. •Small, friendly headquarters where everyone matters. •Travel throughout California as needed (approximately 5-10% of time) •Free parking. What Is this Job? At CSD, the Associate Governmental Program Analyst is a critical, highly visible position:
•Develop the biennial State Plan and Application, Community Action Plan (CAP) documents, and all contracts within the CSDiv. •Complete and submit the CSBG Information System (CSBG/IS) Survey. •Develop program analysis and evaluation tools to assess the compliance and outcomes of the CSDiv programs. •Coordinate with the Field Operations Unit the development and update of the on-site monitoring and desk review tools. •Coordinate with the Field Operations Unit the analysis and evaluation tools for CSDiv work products. •Research and draft recommendations, policies, and procedures. •Develop ad hoc outcome reports, outcome status reports, and provide technical assistance to contractors. •Conduct surveys utilizing appropriate survey tools and methods to collect data on the CSDiv programs to propose process improvements and policy revisions. •Develop and maintain a resource bank of model tools and policies for use by the CSDiv contractors in the implementation of their programs. •Develop and/or revise the state's CSBG regulations. •Develop Request for Proposals (RFP's) to solicit proposals. •Develop and maintain updates of training material in accordance with Federal and State laws and regulations; and conduct training. •Statewide travel as necessary (approximately 5-10% of time). •Act as lead on special projects. •Conduct research on state and federal legislative issues and develop recommendations. •Research, aggregate, and prepare program information in response to legislative and other inquiries. •Prepare legislative analysis and reports/Issue memos. •Provide periodic reviews and analyses of current legislation impacting the department and the contractor network. •Develop position papers on specific legislative initiatives. Who is CSD Looking For? The ideal candidate will be a self-starter who has the following desired qualifications, first-hand experience and characteristics: Experience, Knowledge and Skills: •2-3 years of experience conducting analysis and research projects/assignments. •Specific knowledge of the Community Services Block Grant and/or related programs. •Experience administering federal and state funded programs. •Experience with interpreting and implementing requirements of federal and state grants. •Experience with

Notice: If you are not a current or former State employee, you must first take an examination to obtain list eligibility. This does not apply to Student Assistant vacancies. Learn all about it.

Equal Opportunity to all regardless of race, color, creed, national origin, ancestry, sex, marital status, disability, religious or political affiliation, age, or sexual orientation.

It is the objective of the State of California to achieve a drug-free state workplace. Any applicant for State employment will be expected to behave in accordance with this objective because the use of illegal drugs is inconsistent with the law of the State, the rules governing civil service, and the special trust placed in public servants.

How to Get a State Job

developing training material and delivering training to internal and external customers. •Knowledge or familiarity with local government and nonprofit management. •Strong word processing, presentation and spreadsheet skills. Familiarity with databases and web applications. •Strong writing, analytical and project management skills. Characteristics: •Leadership - Possesses a natural ability and keen desire to manage projects and mentor and guide staff, as well as internal and external customers. Demonstrates and encourages creativity and proactive problem solving. •Credibility and Integrity - Understands internal and external customers and has a true desire to build credibility. Has a personal compass composed of clear principles and the flexibility to balance between literal adherence to rules and the use of policy as a guide. Has the ability to make decisions and be accountable for those decisions. •Teamwork - Cooperates to achieve the department's mission, vision and goals by leading and actively contributing to intradepartmental project teams. •Vision - Understands the context and mission of the Department both internal and external. Has an awareness of the Department's critical issues, and anticipates and influences the future. Has the ability to organize for success. •Staff Development - To best serve both our internal and external customers, CSD's management team reflects, understands and is sensitive to the diversity of the people we serve. SUMMARY OF RESPONSIBILITIES: •Under the direction of the Staff Services Manager I, Program Development and Technical Support Unit (PDTS), the AGPA is part of a team that is responsible for the effective administration of the Community Services Divisions (CSDiv) programs. The programs include the Community Services Block Grant (CSBG) and other federal and state community services funded programs. The AGPA will perform in a lead capacity on a variety of technical and analytical duties, and will be responsible for the more difficult or sensitive assignments. The AGPA may be assigned to monitor and evaluate contractors to ensure compliance with the provisions of Federal and State laws and regulations and contract, and will be expected to travel throughout California as needed (approximately 5-10% of time). Please see the Duty Statement at http://www.csd.ca.gov for a detailed list of the essential and related functions of this position. SELECTION CRITERIA Persons currently appointed to a permanent, full-time Associate Governmental Program Analyst or persons with list eligibility or eligibility for lateral transfer may apply. Please clearly state your eligibility in Section 12 of the application (Std. 678) and attach a copy of your test score notice. All applications must include a Statement of Qualifications clearly demonstrating your knowledge, experience, skills, education level and other characteristics that make you a great fit for the position. All appointments will be made in accordance with The Governor's Executive Order S-09-08, Department of Finance freeze exemption policies, and the State Personnel Board and Department of Personnel Administration laws, rules, regulations, and policies.

Additional Information:

Working Title	Position Number
Associate Governmental Program Analyst	016 - 255 - 5393 - XX
Location	County
Sacramento	SACRAMENTO
Timebase	Tenure
Full Time	Permanent month(s)
Final Filing Date:	Department Link:
Until Filled	None Specified
Contact Unit/Address	Contact Name/Phone
Human Resources P.O. Box 1947 Sacramento, CA 95812-1947	Lynette Pacheco (916) 576-5297 lpacheco@csd.ca.gov

Use your browsers "BACK" button to return to your results/listing page.

Start A New Search